WOMEN
IN HISTORY

WOMEN AND POLITICS

Ann Kramer

Wayland

WOMEN
IN HISTORY

Women and Business
Women and Education
Women and Literature
Women and Politics
Women in Science and Technology
Women and Sport
Women and the Arts
Women and the Family
Women and War
Women and Work

Series editor: Amanda Earl
Consultant: Deirdre Beddoe BA, PhD, Dip Ed,
Reader in History at The Polytechnic of Wales
Designer: Joyce Chester
Picture editors: Jane Marrow and Liz Miller

The author would like to thank Judy Clark and Eileen Yeo for their help.

Front cover: Millicent Garrett Fawcett, president of the National Union of Women's Suffrage Societies, speaking at meeting in Hyde Park in 1913.
Back cover: Top left – Josephine Butler, social reformer. Top right – Orange seller's deputation to the Home Office, 1914. Bottom left – Women campaigning to gain the vote at the age of 21, July 1927. Bottom right – Greenham Women's Peace Camp, 1982.

First published in 1988 by
Wayland (Publishers) Limited
61 Western Road, Hove
East Sussex, BN3 1JD, England

© Copyright 1988 Wayland (Publishers) Limited

British Library Cataloguing in Publication Data
Kramer, Ann
    Women and politics. – (Women in history).
    1. Politics. Role of women, 1850–1986
    I. Title II. Series
    323.3'4'0904

    ISBN 1-85210-388-4

Typeset by Butler & Tanner Ltd
Printed and bound in Great Britain by
Butler & Tanner Ltd, Frome and London

Picture acknowledgements
The pictures in this book were supplied by the following: Aldus Archive 12 (below), 25; Ann Ronan 14, 20 (above), 28; Barnaby's Picture Library 33 (above), 38–9; BBC Hulton Picture Library back cover (bottom left), 7, 9, 13 (below), 20 (below) 27, 29 (below), 30 (below), 31 (above), 34, 35, 37, 40 (above); The Fawcett Library 11; Format 4 (below); Girton College Archives 15 (below); John Gorman Collection 17 (left), 30 (above), 44; The Labour Party 43; The Mansell Collection back cover (top right), 10 (below), 15 (inset), 23; Mary Evans Picture Library front cover, back cover (top left), 10 (above), 12 (above), 13 (above), 16, 17 (right), 18, 19 (both), 21 (both), 24, 36; National Portrait Gallery 8; The Science Museum 5 (bottom right); The SLD Party 42; Syndication International 37 (above); Topham back cover (bottom right), 40 (below), 41 (both). The remaining pictures are from Wayland Picture Library. The publishers would also like to thank The Fawcett Library for all their help and co-operation.

Permissions
The publishers would like to thank the following for permitting the use of certain extracts in the quotations: Age Exchange Publications for *What did you do in the War, Mum?*; J. M. Dent & Sons for Mary Wollstonecraft's *Vindication of the Rights of Women*; Virago Press for William Thompson's *An Appeal of One Half of the Human Race, Women, against the Pretensions of the Other Half, Men,* and Hannah Mitchell's *The Hard Way Up*; The Women's Press for *Greenham Common: Women at the Wire.*

Contents

Above Nancy Astor, Britain's first woman Member of Parliament, at her declaration in November 1919.

6

I myself have never been able to find out precisely what feminism is; I only know that people call me a feminist whenever I express sentiments that differentiate me from a doormat . . .' Rebecca West, writer, 1913.

9

Below Diane Abbott, Britain's first black woman MP at her declaration in June 1987.

Introduction

In 1979, Margaret Thatcher became Britain's first woman Prime Minister. Fifty-one years after the vote had been granted to all adult women in Britain, a woman had finally reached the highest political office in the land.

Today, women can be seen in all areas of political life, from local and central government to 'grass-root' activities. They are Members of Parliament and trade union officials, mayoresses, peeresses and campaigners.

This book examines women's involvement in many areas of politics from the early nineteenth century to the present day; from the spontaneous bread riots in 1812 to the more organized campaigns for women's suffrage and parliamentary representation in the late nineteenth and early twentieth centuries. It also looks at the evolution of feminism, and the development of the early women's movement, with its impact on a wide range of issues: work conditions and opportunities, property rights, health and contraception, for example.

With the rise of the modern women's movement in the late 1960s, women began to delve back into the past and, not surprisingly, found that women's political involvement has a long and fascinating history. Until recently, much of women's involvement has been 'hidden from history', and to some extent ignored. Some historians have trivialized the role women have played, or have concentrated only on a few well-known names. As a result, most people have heard of the Pankhursts and their suffragette followers, many of whom went to prison during their long campaign to win votes for women. But far fewer know about the work of, for example, the Women's Co-operative Guild, which fought for the rights of married working-class women, and did so much to win maternity benefits.

This book evaluates the mixed success of women in changing the political climate for the better. In 1988, Margaret Thatcher became the longest standing Prime Minister in Britain this century, but still the British Parliament contained only 41 women out of a total of 650. This book investigates what more needs to be done before all women are treated as equals with men, and before the law.

1

'The Perfect Lady'

Beginnings are always hard to find and this is as true of the beginnings of women's involvement in politics, as it is of any other historical study. In 1792, a remarkable woman called Mary Wollstonecraft wrote and published *Vindication of the Rights of Woman*. In the book she argued that if women had the gift of reason, they should be treated equally with men. Mary Wollstonecraft was not the first to challenge male power, or to demand rights for women, nor was she alone. But her book is one of the most important expressions of feminist ideas, and a starting point for feminism in Britain.

Ideas alone do not make change, however. The enormous social and economic upheaval happening in Britain at this time also influenced values and beliefs. The Industrial Revolution, which began in the early 1760s, had brought great changes to the way in which goods were produced. Power-driven machinery, tended by fewer workers, took over from the slower home-based crafts. The shift from cottage-based industry to factory-based industrial production was rapid.

Industrialization brought with it a devaluing of the economic importance of women's work. The factories required cheap labour to operate machinery, and vast numbers of women and children were employed for such purposes. Their work was hard, and their wages were extremely low. For many working women, the introduction of

Above *The 'perfect lady'. A stereotypical idea of the family was encouraged among the middle classes in Victorian Britain— the husband as breadwinner, with dependent wife and children.*

Below left *Working-class women and children working at home. In pre-industrial Britain, the home was the centre of work and family life.*

Below *Industrialization brought many changes. In the early nineteenth century women and children provided employers with cheap labour in the factories.*

' *Confined . . . in cages like the feathered race, they have nothing to do but to plume themselves, and stalk with mock majesty from perch to perch. It is true they are provided with food and raiment, for which they neither toil nor spin, but health, liberty and virtue are given in exchange.* Mary Wollstonecraft's view of women's position in society, from *Vindication of the Rights of Woman*, 1792. **'**

' *His intellect is for invention; his energy for adventure, for war, and for conquest . . . But the women's power is . . . not for battle – and her intellect is not for invention or creation . . . Her great function is Praise.* John Ruskin, *Sesame and Lilies*, 1865. **'**

Until 1842, women worked underground in the mines of industrial Britain. It was impossible for them to follow the 'perfect-lady' lifestyle. They had to work to survive.

the factory system meant an end to the old system of home-based work, in which all members of the family played a part. Instead, home and work became separated, leaving working-class women with the double task of factory work and domestic work.

Not all women went out to work, however. As industrialization continued, some married women took to doing paid work at home – sewing, taking in washing, childminding, lace making and so on. It was very different from the family craft work done some fifty years earlier. Homeworking conditions were often appalling, and pay was usually on a 'piece-rate' basis. That is, payment for goods completed, not an hourly rate of pay. Women often had to work 15–16 hours to earn just enough to exist.

The late eighteenth and early nineteenth centuries also saw the development of a distinct middle class. This new class included business men, professional people and wealthy farmers, who believed firmly in the values of progress and hard work.

Central also to the view of this new middle class was a belief in the sanctity and importance of the family. A stereotype family was encouraged among the middle classes – the male as breadwinner, with home-based dependent wife, and children. This idea of the family was also encouraged for the working and upper class. Most people at this time believed that women were intellectually and physically inferior to men, and as the nineteenth century went on, this view of women became stronger.

Within the middle-class stereotype family, the wife was the centre of the home; 'the angel in the home', as the Victorian poet Coventry Patmore described her. Hers was the 'private sphere' – the world of the home in which she was supposed to be the perfect lady, the perfect wife, and the perfect mother. Her husband's sphere, by contrast, was the 'public sphere' – the harsh, outside world of industrial Britain with its factories, coal mines, squalor and poverty. This was the sphere that women were being 'protected' from.

The idea of 'the perfect lady' was widely written about in the poetry and literature of the time. The art critic, John Ruskin, lectured on the subject in 1864. Later, printed in the book *Sesame and Lilies*,

TREMENDOUS SACRIFICE!

the lecture portrayed woman as man's helpmate, a being that made his life complete. Man was the doer of great deeds; the purpose of woman was to praise!

However, in real life the 'perfect lady' lifestyle applied to only a handful of women – those with the money and servants to make it a reality. It did not apply to the large numbers of single women in British society. Nor did it apply to the vast numbers of working women, whose lives were ones of unceasing drudgery in the mines, mills and workshops of the new industrial Britain.

Although the stereotype only applied to a very small group, it was very influential. It was a measure by which women's behaviour was judged, and an ideal which all women were encouraged to try their best to achieve. Soon, however, some middle-class women began to challenge the ideal. They gradually began to criticize their lives of inactivity and their total economic dependence on men.

For working-class women, the situation was different. The effect of the harsh economic conditions of industrialization were crippling to women and their families. They protested against appalling working conditions and pay, and the exploitation of their lives.

Women who did piece-work, or worked in sweatshops, often worked 16 hours a day. Their plight was usually not recognized. In this Victorian cartoon, the overseer relentlessly exploits women's labour, while the 'ladies' in the shop outside are oblivious to the working conditions.

❛

A woman's highest duty is so often to suffer and be still. Sarah Stickney Ellis, *The Women of England*. 1845.

❜

Mary Wollstonecraft (1759–1797)

Mary Wollstonecraft was an eighteenth century feminist, radical thinker and writer. Her work *Vindication of the Rights of Woman*, published in 1792, is one of the most influential pieces of feminist writing in history.

Mary recognized the oppression of women from an early age. She was from an upper-class family, and was the second of seven children. Against all odds, Mary managed to educate herself, but was forced to support her family and herself, working as either a companion, governess or teacher. It was poorly-paid work, but it was the only work considered suitable for a woman of her class.

After her mother's death in 1782, Mary, together with her sister Eliza and close friend Fanny Blood, opened a school for girls. Mary did this because she felt girls were caught in a vicious circle. They were not given the same educational opportunities as men, and therefore appeared less 'academic' and intelligent. This then gave the impression that men were right and that women were not worth educating!

The school unfortunately failed, but through it Mary became part of a group of well-known radical thinkers called the 'English Jacobins'. The members of the group, which included the economist Tom Paine, and the poet William Blake, set out to try to reform society.

Encouraged by her friends and driven by her beliefs, Mary began to write (an occupation frowned on by many men and women of the time). She published her first book *Thoughts on the Education of Daughters* in 1787, and *Vindication of the Rights of Woman* five years later. In this book, Mary made a passionate plea for equal rights for women. She bitterly criticized the fact that women of her class were expected to be 'the toys of man [who] must jingle in his ears whenever, dismissing reason, he chooses to be amused'. She argued that women were not 'naturally' weak, but that their inferior position was due to the way in which they were treated as personal slaves by men.

Views such as these, at a time when women were supposed to be the 'angel in the home', did not endear Mary to many people. Her book caused a considerable stir, and only a small circle of friends agreed with her. Most people attacked her ideas bitterly, and she was described by one critic as a 'hyena in petticoats'.

Mary Wollstonecraft's unconventional lifestyle was often criticized as much as her outspoken views. She had a number of love affairs and an illegitimate child, which caused quite a scandal.

2

The Early Years

1800-1840

The early years of the nineteenth century were turbulent ones as the effects of industrialization began to be felt in Britain. High prices for food, low wages and poverty, led to outbursts of protest, mass demonstrations, and the growth of some new radical political movements. In all forms of political protest, women were very much involved.

Traditionally, women were responsible for feeding the family and during the late eighteenth and early nineteenth centuries, women played a major part in the many bread riots caused by high prices and scarcity of corn. In Nottingham in 1812, for instance, a dramatic protest against the the high price of bread — the staple diet of the poor — was staged by angry women who dyed a loaf of bread red, tied it with black cloth and stuck it on top of a fishing rod as a symbol of the 'bleeding famine' affecting so many poor families at that time.

High prices, however, were not the only cause of protest. The new machinery itself caused great hardship, particularly among the handloom weavers, who faced starvation as they were thrown out of work. Machine breaking was a common way of protesting, and women supported such actions. The introduction of the hated New Poor Law in 1834 (which meant that poor people, who could find no work, had to enter a workhouse before they received any assistance) also caused protest. Women led many of the outbursts and demonstrations against the new laws, which in effect separated children from parents and wives from husbands by placing them in separate workhouses.

As the century continued, this sort of traditional protest was channelled more and more into either the setting up of trade unions or the forming of new political movements. Both types of organizing raised the question of women's 'right' to actually become involved in politics.

In 1824 the Combination Acts that had been introduced in 1799 and 1800 to prevent workers from organizing themselves into unions, were repealed. As a result, the period from 1824 to 1850 saw a burst of trade union activity. Organization was strongest in the new factories.

Above *An early trade union membership card for the Power Loom Female Weavers Society. It is dated 1833. With the repeal of the Combination Acts in 1824, there was a burst of trade union activity.*

' *We have been told that the province of woman is her home, and that the field of politics should be left to men; this we deny ... Is it not true that the interests of our fathers, husbands and brothers, ought to be ours? If they are oppressed and impoverished, do we not share those evils with them?* Female Political Union, Newcastle-on-Tyne, 1839. **'**

Right The Corn Laws of 1815 caused great hardship for working people. The laws kept the price of bread high by preventing imports of cheaper foreign corn. Women played a major part in the demonstrations against these laws, which became known as the 'bread riots'.

❛

We may sigh for the conditions of women ... but until we secure our own rights of citizenship we can do nothing for them. From *The Destructive and Poor Man's Conservative*, 1834.

❜

Below A contemporary print of the Peterloo Massacre in 1819. Women were involved in the fight for Parliamentary reform.

For married working women, involvement in union activities presented many problems – a long strike meant hardship and hunger for the family, yet women felt very strongly about supporting their workmates. Women's presence in trade unions, however, was often resented by many male workers who feared competition at work from lower-paid women doing the same work. Male workers said they needed more money because they had to support themselves and a family. No one seemed concerned about single working women, who received low wages, and did not have a husband's wage to help.

Despite these problems, working women did join unions, and also took part in strike action. In Leeds in 1833, for example, 1,500 women who worked in the woollen mills came out on strike, an action which was regarded with horror by the middle classes who were not only frightened of unions, but also feared that such independent action by women would threaten the very basis of society.

Women were also involved in the short-lived Grand National Consolidated Trade Union (GNCTU). The GNCTU was formed in 1834, and attempted to combine all trade unions into one strong group. Women were represented in the unions of the Operative Bonnet Makers, the Female Tailors, and as Women of Britain and Ireland. The GNCTU collapsed through lack of funds and generally women then remained outside trade unions until later in the century.

Women were drawn into more radical politics too. From the early 1800s, increasing numbers of people were demanding the reform of Parliament and the right to have a say in government through gaining the vote. The first Female Reform Society was formed in Lancashire in 1818 and women were among the victims of the 1819 Peterloo Massacre, when government cavalry troops charged a peaceful meeting of reform supporters in St Peter's Fields, Manchester. Eleven people were killed and 400 men, women and children were injured.

In 1832, the vote was granted to middle-class men. Working people who had fought for reform felt betrayed, and the late 1830s saw the emergence of a new movement – Chartism. This was based around the Great Charter with its demands for parliamentary reform. The Charter included a demand for votes for all men and women over 21. Other demands were a secret ballot, annual parliaments, no property qualifications for MPs, payment for MPs and equal voting constituencies.

The movement drew in thousands of working-class people throughout the country, and although later petitions dropped the reference to women, it has been estimated that women formed at least 80 Chartist associations between 1837 and 1844. Chartist women marched, attended rallies, and petitioned Parliament. As social conditions began to improve in the late 1840s, Chartism seemed to 'run out of steam', but it did eventually give way to new and stronger forms of workers' organizations.

Many of the early political movements did not look specifically at women's rights. Yet, working-class women saw that their situation was similar to that of men and they helped to attack the injustices of industralization that destroyed their lives.

One strand of politics, however, did look at the position of women in society. Known as Owenite socialism, it was built on an idea of a society based on co-operation and mutual help rather than on competition and self-interest.

The movement was influenced by the writings of Mary Wollstonecraft and the work of Robert Owen, who had introduced welfare benefits, schooling and housing for workers in his cotton mill in New Lanark, Scotland. The movement disagreed with the existing basis of society, and in particular marriage and the family, which were seen to be oppressive to women. They believed in complete equality between men and women.

At its height, the ideals of Owenite socialism attracted large numbers of followers, many of them women from the upper working- and lower middle-classes. Women such as Anna Wheeler, held meetings, organized lectures and wrote articles on women's rights and women's issues. She is remembered in *An Appeal of One Half of the Human Race, Women, against the Pretensions of the Other Half, Men,* by William Thompson. Published in 1825, *Appeal* was a scathing attack on male control over women and it is an important political work. The book carried Thompson's name as author, but he dedicated it to Anna Wheeler and credited her with the chief responsibility for its views.

Hundreds of women attended Owenite lectures and meetings, but as the economic climate began to improve this movement collapsed too in 1845, to be replaced by other forms of socialism.

> *Awake, arise, shake off these fetters ... To obtain equal rights ... you must be respected by [men]; not merely desired, like rare meat, to pamper their selfish appetites ... Assert your right as human beings to equal individual liberty, to equal laws ... to equal morals, to equal education – and, as a result of the whole, to equal chances.*
> William Thompson, *An Appeal of One Half of the Human Race, Women, against the Pretensions of the Other Half, Men,* 1825.

A portrait of Anna Wheeler.

THE
ENGLISH WOMAN'S JOURNAL.

PUBLISHED MONTHLY.

VOL. III.   June 1, 1859.   No. 16.

XXXVI.—THE DETAILS OF WOMAN'S WORK IN
SANITARY REFORM.

"I conclude that all our endowments for social good, whatever their
especial purpose or denomination, educational, sanitary, charitable, penal—
will prosper and fulfil their objects in so far as we carry out the principle of
combining in due proportion the masculine and the feminine element, and
will fail or become perverted into some form of evil in so far as we neglect
or ignore it."
                                        Mrs. Jameson.

SANITARY REFORM is an object claiming the most serious attention
of every conscientious woman. We, the inhabitants of this wonderful
little England, have attained to a height of civilization beyond that
of any other people; but it is a lamentable fact that the improvement
in our physical condition is far from being commensurate with our
general progress. Among us are seen examples of mental and
moral dignity, equalled by few of the most advanced nations; but
among us also exist physical degradation and suffering unknown to
many of the most savage tribes; to all the blessings of Christian
civilization our children are heirs, but a third of them die before
they can enjoy their heritage.* Our productions win for us wo

The English Woman's Journal, first published in 1857, was an important mouthpiece for the early discussions of women's involvement in politics and women's rights.

What have I done this last fortnight? I have read the 'Daughter at Home' to father, and two chapters of 'Mackintosh'; a volume of 'Sybil' to Mama. Learnt seven tunes by heart, written various letters ... Paid eight visits. Done company. And that is all.'
Florence Nightingale, extract from her diary, 1846.

Right Florence Nightingale at her hospital in Scutari in the Crimea during the Crimean War. She had to fight against opposition from her parents and society to make a career for herself in nursing.

3

Middle-class women begin to rebel

1840-1870

While working women protested against the effects of industrialization, middle-class women too were beginning to rebel. There were no organized women's feminist groups in Britain before 1850, but rebellion could be clearly seen in individuals. Some, such as Charlotte Brontë, turned to writing, and in novels like *Shirley* (published in 1849), expressed the frustration that women of middle class felt about being financially dependent on men. Florence Nightingale was another woman who longed to work and have a career — an idea which the majority of middle-class women found shocking. She protested bitterly against the futility of her idle life, and against much opposition went on to make nursing a respected occupation for women.

Some middle-class women became involved in the political campaigns of the time, such as the anti-slavery movement. They usually played a background role, and did little more than raise funds. In 1853, for instance, the Bristol and Clifton Ladies' Anti-Slavery Society advertised for a man to organize their public meetings, as it was considered 'unsuitable' for women to do such things! However, any sort of involvement gave women much needed political experience, which would be useful later. Importantly, some women also began to make a connection between the position of slaves, who were regarded as property, and the position of women.

By law, in Britain in the early nineteenth century, women were the property of men. They were described as 'femmes couverts',

Left *As this view of an anti-slavery meeting in 1841 shows, women mainly took supporting roles in the abolition campaign. Speakers and meeting organizers were all men.*

which meant that they were under the control of their fathers, or, if married, their husbands. A single woman had few legal rights; once she was married, she had none at all. Her body, her clothing and all her personal property belonged to her husband. Even children from the marriage were her husband's sole property.

A number of women were beginning to challenge such an unfair situation. The first public battle happened in the 1830s, when Caroline Norton, an aristocratic woman who had separated from her drunken husband, campaigned to gain the right to visit her children. She wrote pamphlets, petitioned Parliament and won considerable public support. In 1839, the Infants' Custody Bill was passed. It only gave women limited access to visit their children, but it was very important in paving the way for further change.

In 1854, a woman named Barbara Bodichon began a wider protest for the rights of married women, including the right to own property and make a will. She wrote a pamphlet and drew up a petition asking for financial independence for women. The petition was signed by 26,000 women and men, and in 1857, a Married Women's Property Bill went before Parliament. The bill was not passed, but a second bill, the Marriage and Divorce Bill, was passed instead. This, at least, enabled women who separated from their husbands to keep any property inherited or money earned after the separation.

By the 1850s, a small, but now famous group of feminists was emerging. It included Barbara Bodichon, Emily Davies, campaigner for higher education for girls and Elizabeth Garrett, the first British woman doctor. They opened offices in Langham Place, London, and in 1857 founded the *English Woman's Journal*. This magazine was to become a well-known mouthpiece for the discussion of women's politics and women's rights.

The right to be allowed to work, and receive an adequate education, were among their main concerns. The census of 1851 had shown that

> **'** **By marriage the very being or legal existence of a woman is suspended, or at least it is incorporated ... into that of her husband, under whose wing, protection and cover she performs everything.** William Blackstone, *Commentary on the Laws of England*, 1765 **'**

Elizabeth Garrett, the first British woman doctor also campaigned for the improvement of women's rights.

THE ANGEL IN 'THE HOUSE;'" OR, THE RESULT OF FEMALE SUFFRAGE.

Above A cartoon in Punch *magazine in 1884 reflects conventional society's fears of what would happen to women if they gained the vote.*

6
Give some women votes, and it will tend to make all women think seriously of the concerns of the nation at large ... There is no reason why women should not take an active interest in all the social questions ... which occupy Parliament. Barbara Bodichon, *Reasons For and Against the Enfranchisement of Women, 1866.*
9

women outnumbered men by about one million. Obviously, many women therefore could not marry as society expected them to, and yet the only 'acceptable' jobs for single middle-class women were those of governess or milliner. The 'Ladies of Langham Place', as the group became known, set out to open up education, the professions and the 'public sphere' to women.

It was a long and difficult struggle. The barriers were enormous, and their efforts were met with hostility from the press, the medical profession and academics. But, the women of Langham Place pressed on, and inspired many others to join them. Their offices were a hive of activity, and for the first time the beginnings of an organized movement to promote equal rights for women could be seen.

The Langham Place women were very influential. They looked at both the legal and economic discrimination women faced. They also exposed the hypocrisy in a society that said a woman's place was in the home, but then forced one class of women to work in appalling conditions in factories.

More and more, women's right to vote was seen as a key to being able to change things. If women could vote and have a voice in Parliament, then they could change 'man'-made laws and injustices.

The views of the women of Langham Place were quite shocking for the time. Many opponents of women's suffrage (the right to vote) said that women were unfit to vote, and that they could easily be represented by men. They also argued that it would not be 'suitable' for women to become involved in politics.

The 1832 Reform Bill had given the vote to middle-class male householders, but had excluded working-class men. By the 1860s, working-class men again became impatient to gain the vote. Some women hoped that they too might be included in a new Reform Bill which was to be read in Parliament. Women had to rely on sympathetic MPs to put their case, as they had no other way of expressing their views in Parliament. They found a champion in John Stuart Mill, who was a strong supporter of women's rights.

A petition was drawn up by Barbara Bodichon, and within two weeks some 1,500 signatures were obtained. In 1867, Mill presented the petition to the House of Commons. In a long and reasoned speech, he asked that suitably qualified women (single women householders and widows) should be included in the Reform Bill then being discussed. It was the very first time that the question of votes for women had been mentioned in Parliament, and it caused such a stir that many MPs gave up other engagements to be there. Although the amendment would have only given the vote to a small number of well-to-do single women and widows, it was instantly defeated. The 1867 Reform Bill agreed to give the vote to male householders and tenants, but it still excluded women.

Barbara Bodichon (1827–1891)

Barbara Bodichon was an active campaigner in the fight for married women's property rights and a leading force in the creation of the nineteenth century women's movement.

Barbara was born into a wealthy and radical family and was first cousin to Florence Nightingale. Her mother died when she was young and Barbara was forced to take over the running of the household. When she was 21, her father provided her with an annual income of £300 which, unlike most other women, enabled her to live an independent life.

In 1854, she wrote and published *A Brief Summary in Plain Language of the most important Laws concerning Women*. It set out for the first time the full extent of how the legal system discriminated against women. To have produced such a document was, in itself, quite unusual for a woman, but Barbara was also a lively and energetic campaigner, who fought to change many unjust laws. She is most well-known for the submission of the Married Women's Property Bill, which went before Parliament in 1857.

She produced another pamphlet, *Women and Work*, in which she made a scathing attack on the popular view that women were made only for men's amusement, and argued forcefully for equal opportunities, adequately paid work, and proper training for women. She later went on, with the help of other women, to form the first Women's Suffrage Committee in Britain in the 1860s. The views of Barbara Bodichon and the 'Ladies of Langham Place' were greeted with scorn and hostility by the British press. Critics advised them either to marry, or 'hold their tongues in a dignified manner'. But, Barbara was too determined and intelligent a woman to be put off by harsh words.

Her independent income put her in a privileged position, but she had a life-long commitment to equal rights for women, and believed that women of her class should be given responsibility and a place outside of the home. Her enthusiasm and untiring work were an inspiration to many women.

Inset *Barbara Bodichon, one of the original 'Ladies of Langham Place'.*

Below *Girton College, Cambridge. Bodichon was inspirational in the founding of this college for women.*

Above Josephine Butler headed the first women-only political organization to fight the Contagious Diseases Acts.

4

Protest and Reform

1870-1890

By the 1870s, women were demanding changes in many aspects of society. Middle-class women, such as Emily Davies continued to demand higher and university education for women, while Elizabeth Garrett and Sophia Jex-Blake spearheaded women's entrance into medical training. Their efforts were met by constant ridicule and opposition, but one campaign in particular shocked Victorian feelings completely, and even shocked many feminist supporters.

This campaign of protest, which horrified so many people, was against the Contagious Diseases Acts. These acts had been introduced in the 1870s in military towns where soldiers were stationed. The acts related to prostitutes. Under the acts, any woman suspected of being a prostitute could be arrested and subjected to an unpleasant medical examination. If a woman was found to be suffering from a venereal disease, she was imprisoned in a special hospital for anything up to nine months.

In 1869, the Ladies' National Association (LNA), was formed to fight these acts. It was headed by a remarkable woman, Josephine Butler, and was the very first women-only political organization in Britain. It began its campaign with a public protest in the *Daily News* newspaper, signed by 2,000 women. 'The Women's Protest', as it was known, attacked the acts for their glaring double standard and lack of justice — the acts punished the prostitute, but not her client.

The LNA published an avalanche of propaganda, including a regular newspaper, lobbied Parliament and held public meetings. For the Victorians, sex was a subject that was not discussed at all, and it was quite unthinkable for many people to see the subject being discussed by middle-class 'ladies'. Josephine Butler and the LNA were angrily attacked in the press.

Butler continued to make her point that women became prostitutes because they were very poor, and needed money to live. If they were given training and a good education for a skilled job, they would not need to turn to prostitution. After many years of campaigning, the Contagious Diseases Acts were repealed in 1886. The LNA had won their victory.

From the 1870s, working-class women were also beginning to

❝ I thought ... it was a Parliament of men only who made this law which treats you as an outlaw. Men alone met in committee over it. Men alone are the executives ... it is time that women should arise and demand their most sacred rights in regard to their sisters ... Josephine Butler, *Shield*, March 1870. ❞

organize on a larger scale in trade unions. Again, women unionists had to face a double struggle – the fight to improve their working conditions, and the fight to be accepted by male trade unionists. In 1874, Emma Patterson, the daughter of a school teacher, formed the Women's Provident and Protective League (later to be known as the Women's Trade Union League), with the aim of setting up unions in all the trades where women worked.

In 1875, Patterson became the first woman to attend the Trades Union Congress (TUC). The first branch of the League was founded in Bristol, and by the 1890s, the League had more than 30 branches in dress-making, book-binding, millinery and other trades. It was the earliest organization to fight solely for working women, and it encouraged the formation of many more small unions for women throughout the country.

The League acted as a mouthpiece for women workers, and also campaigned to change the attitudes of male workers towards women in industry. As industrialization continued, many skilled male workers set up membership rules to protect their jobs. More and more women were being excluded from doing skilled work. As some skilled work was becoming less and less physically demanding, due to advances in machinery, women were quite capable of doing it – if only they were given the chance.

Protective legislation was introduced, which stopped women from doing some skilled jobs. It was said that such measures were taken to 'protect' women's health and wellbeing against dangerous machinery for example, but to a great extent it was to stop them from working where they might be in competition with men. In 1842, women were banned from working underground in the mining industry, and the Factory Acts of the same year, made married women give up certain work. Women were also excluded from night work,

Above Strike action by women workers to gain better pay and working conditions increased in the latter half of the nineteenth century. This illustration shows overground workers leaving the coal mines during a strike in South Wales in 1873.

Above left From the 1870s, women were becoming much more involved in trade unions. This banner of 1882 sums up the demands of working women—Equality, Fraternity and Liberty.

❝ *... It was their duty as men and husbands to use their utmost efforts to bring about a condition of things where their wives should be in their proper sphere at home, seeing after their house and family, instead of being dragged into the competition for livelihood against the great and strong men of the world ...* Mr Broadhurst, Trades Union Congress, 1877. **❞**

COLLIERY LASSES

Protective legislation sought to limit the type of work done by women. Pit-brow lassies (like those above) worked on the surface of the mines. They successfully challenged attempts to stop them working in the mines during the 1880s and 1890s.

and could only do limited amounts of overtime. The question of limiting women's work in this way, was a major issue which the Women's Trade Union League fought against. Protective legislation reached its peak in the 1880s with an attempt to remove the pit-brow lassies (who worked on the surface of the mines), from the mining industry altogether. The legislation failed after the pit-brow lassies made a deputation to Parliament, but women were constantly fighting to maintain and safeguard work opportunities.

From the late 1880s, until about 1892, there was an upsurge in militant activity among unskilled workers, both men and women. Early actions included the famous matchgirls' strike in London in 1888. Bryant and May's employees worked long hours in dangerous conditions. The young girls and women had to make the matches by hand, dipping them in a dangerous chemical called phosphorous. This caused a terrible disease called 'phossy jaw', which ate away at their teeth and jaw bone. Their wages were very low and were further reduced by fines, if they made any mistakes.

Through reading an article in a socialist newspaper called *The Link*, the matchgirls were inspired to strike for better pay and conditions.

> **6**
>
> *These 'female hands' eat their food in the rooms in which they work . . . the phosphorus works on them as they chew their food, and rots away the bone. The foremen have sharp eyes. If they see a girl's face swell . . . she is sent off and gets no pay. White Slavery, The Link, 1888.*
>
> **9**

With the help of the editor of the paper, Annie Besant, they won many improvements. Their success made it clear to other workers, that unity could bring with it considerable power. The same year also saw strikes by women blanket weavers in Yorkshire, women cigar makers in Nottingham, cotton and jute workers in Dundee, and mill girls in Kilmarnock. Their actions not only forced employers to pay better wages, and improve conditions, but also forced trade unionists to take women more seriously.

While women were organizing at work, women at home had no one to speak for them. In 1883, The Women's Co-operative Guild was formed. It was very important as it was the first British women's organization run by working-class women. It began when a section in the paper *Co-operative News*, entitled 'Women's Corner', wrote about issues affecting working-class women.

Initially, the Guild was small, but by 1892 it had some 4,000–5,000 members in 98 branches throughout the country. It quickly expanded its interests from domestic matters to include political

Left *The Bryant and May matchgirls' strike was to become very famous in the history of women's involvement in politics. This picture shows the strike committee, with Annie Besant at the centre of the table.*

Striking matchgirls outside their factory in 1888.

issues, women's rights, birth control and child welfare. For married working-class women, the Guild provided education, experience in public speaking and an opportunity to work out ideas and campaigns. It was a highly influential, respected organization and did a great deal of work to publicize the problems of women, particularly in areas such as maternity.

Gradually, women all over the country, in different social classes, were gaining influence and independence. In 1888, women house-holders were given the right to vote in elections for the newly formed county councils. During the 1880's, the Conservative Primrose League was formed, and in 1886 Mrs Gladstone (Prime Minister William Gladstone's wife) set up the Women's Liberal Federation to 'help our husbands'. But, the right to vote in Parliamentary elections remained as far away as ever. By 1890, after two decades of petition-ing, campaigning and letter writing, no real progress had been made; the fight for women's suffrage had reached stalemate.

Furthermore, the suffrage campaign was also divided over the issue of which women should have the vote. Lydia Becker, who headed the women's suffrage campaign for twenty years, wanted to restrict the vote to unmarried rate-paying women. Others wanted the vote for married women as well, while some wanted 'universal suffrage', the vote for all women and men over 21 years of age. Opposition to any one of these demands still remained very fierce. Even Queen Victoria herself commented angrily on the 'mad, wicked folly of women's rights', and in 1889, a *Solemn Protest* against votes for women was published and signed by Mrs Humphrey Ward and other prominent women, who believed that women's rights campaigners had gone far enough. They formed their own Anti-Suffrage League, but the old argument that women should stay out of politics could not be taken seriously – they were already there!

Above *Lydia Becker kept the suffrage issue alive from the 1870s to her death in 1890. In this cartoon she is seen wrapped up in one of the private members' bills which were put before Parliament every year to try and gain women the vote.*

Millicent Fawcett, president of the National Union of Women's Suffrage Societies (NUWSS).

5

The Cause

1890-1914

From the 1890s, the women's suffrage campaign entered a new phase. New Zealand had given women the vote in 1893; South Australia followed in 1894. In 1895, the British general election had returned many MPs sympathetic to women's suffrage. This, plus growing support from working-class women, gave the suffrage campaign new energy.

In the years leading up to 1914, 'the cause' as the fight for the vote became known, drew in thousands of women from all over Britain. It was a remarkable and thrilling period as actresses, shop assistants, clerks, aristocratic women, university students, trade unionists, socialists, Guild women, middle-class and working-class women alike threw themselves into the bitter struggle for women's right to vote.

From 1906 to 1914 long-skirted women everywhere, in the face of hostility and contempt, held meetings, chalked pavements, marched, demonstrated, raised funds and produced propaganda in a campaign that made 'Votes for Women' one of the leading political issues of the day.

There were two main strands. The first and largest, were the suffragists who organized in the National Union of Women's Suffrage Societies (NUWSS). This was set up in 1897 by Millicent Fawcett. It was an 'umbrella' organization, bringing together all the older suffrage societies, as well as attracting new recruits, among them Ada Nield Chew, the experienced union and labour organizer from the north of England. The NUWSS believed in peaceful tactics. It was run on democratic lines, produced its own newspaper, *The Common Cause*, and by 1914 had a membership of nearly 60,000 women in branches throughout the country.

The second strand were the suffragettes, militant women who organized in the Women's Social and Political Union (WSPU). The WSPU was formed in Manchester in 1903 by Emmeline Pankhurst, widow of the radical lawyer Dr Richard Pankhurst, and her two daughters Sylvia, a socialist and artist, and Christabel, a law student.

The aim of the WSPU was 'immediate enfranchisement' by 'political

Above Emmeline Pankhurst was the inspiration behind the founding of the Women's Social and Political Union (WSPU) in 1903. Unlike the NUWSS, the WSPU was a militant union, which chose to confront the government on the issue of votes for women.

Above Left Christabel Pankhurst (2nd left) and Annie Kenney (3rd left) at a WSPU meeting.

action'. From the start the WSPU rejected traditional methods in favour of militancy (warfare). Rather than co-operate with the government, they chose confrontation. They first came to public attention in 1905 when Christabel Pankhurst and Annie Kenney, a young mill worker from Oldham, stood up in the Manchester Free Trade Hall at a Liberal Party election meeting, and asked what was to become a famous question: 'Will the Liberal Party give votes to women?' The hall erupted in uproar. The two young women were arrested. Both refused to pay their fines and were sent to prison.

The next day the newspapers were full of the incident and women's suffrage was finally front-page news. This one event had done more to publicize votes for women than 40 years of more peaceful campaigning.

In 1906, the WSPU moved their headquarters to Clements Inn, London and from then on the suffragettes, as they were known after an insult in the *Daily Mail*, were rarely out of the news.

The WSPU was run like a volunteer army. Led by Christabel, who thought up increasingly dramatic actions, the suffragettes disrupted political meetings, produced an avalanche of propaganda, stormed the House of Commons, and hounded MPs up and down the country. Prime Minister Asquith, a noted opponent of votes for women, was a particular target.

The WSPU attracted large numbers of recruits. Week after week

6

I used to think women could hardly do anything, that it all depended on men. Now it seems that there is nothing brave women cannot do if they are only given the chance. The Women's Outlook, an article in *The Labour Leader*, 1908.

9

Right A suffragette is dragged away by a policeman as she tries to chain herself to the railings of Buckingham Palace.

❝

Militancy is abhored [hated] by me, and the majority of suffragists. None of the great triumphs of the women's movement ... has been won by physical force; ... But militancy has been brought into existence by the blind blundering of politicians who have not understood the women's movement ... people of excitable temperament have been goaded almost to madness by 'shuffling and delay' with which our question has been treated by Parliament ... Millicent Fawcett, 1912.

❞

❝

We are here, not because we are law-breakers; we are here in our efforts to become law-makers'. Emmeline Pankhurst, Bow Street Court, 1908.

❞

❝

Oh Holloway, grim Holloway, With grey forbidding towers! Stern are thy walls, but sterner still Is Woman's free, unconquered will ... Katheleen Emerson, from *Women in Prison,* 1912.

❞

deputations of women led by Emmeline Pankhurst repeatedly tried to get into the House of Commons. Often thousands of police were waiting, and there were violent struggles between suffragettes and police. Women were punched, kicked, their clothes torn, and their breasts twisted viciously. On one occasion in November 1910, later known as Black Friday, 50 women were seriously injured and 2 died after a clash with police that lasted several hours.

Many women were arrested and imprisoned and, from 1909, imprisoned suffragettes went on hunger strike in protest at not being treated as political prisoners. In turn, the government introduced force feeding. The prisoner was held down and a tube was pushed through the nose or mouth into the stomach. Liquid food was then poured down this tube.

There was a public outcry to this form of 'torture' and in 1913 the government introduced the hated 'Cat and Mouse Act'. This meant that starving women were released from prison, only to be re-arrested once their health had improved.

Not all the women agreed with the WSPU's confrontation and militant action. The NUWSS, in contrast, rejected 'militancy' and continued to petition Parliament and to write pamphlets and books explaining why women should have the vote. They also organized massive marches, among them the famous 'mud march' of 1907, when 4,000 women marched from Hyde Park in London, to the Strand in the pouring rain. Another march followed in 1908, when 13,000 women marched from London's Embankment to the Albert Hall.

Other women disagreed with the strict leadership of the WSPU particularly with Emmeline and Christabel Pankhurst. In 1907, Charlotte Despard left the WSPU and set up the Women's Freedom League. The WFL, unlike the WSPU, was run on democratic lines. It too rejected violence. One of its members, Muriel Matters, hired a balloon and showered London with leaflets about women's suffrage. Yet, despite disagreements between the suffrage groups, the different strands frequently worked together and by 1911 it looked as if victory might be in sight.

The newly-formed Labour Party supported votes for women although they were uncertain how it should be achieved. Many Liberals supported the principle too, although a powerful group which included Asquith were strongly opposed. Even so, an all-party committee of the House of Commons met and drew up a Conciliation Bill which would have given votes to women householders and wives of male householders. The suffragettes called a truce and women all over the country waited hopefully. In the end, however, Asquith proposed a bill to enfranchise all men over the age of 21, and the Conciliation Bill was defeated.

Woman suffrage supporters everywhere were angry. In revenge, the suffragettes turned to further violence. In 1912, suffragettes throwing stones broke hundreds of windows in London's East End. As a result, the entire leadership of the WSPU was arrested, except for Christabel, who fled to France to conduct operations from there. Over the next year suffragettes damaged houses, railway stations and other buildings by setting fire to them or blowing them up with home-made bombs.

Tactics such as these lost the support of many people, although even Millicent Fawcett understood that they were caused by years of frustration. By 1914, however, 'votes for women' was becoming less important to the country than the oncoming war with Germany.

White-clothed women in a funeral procession for suffragette Emily Wilding Davison. She died in 1913, after running into the path of King George V's horse at Derby Day, as a protest against prison conditions experienced by suffragettes.

Christabel Pankhurst (1880–1958)

Christabel Pankhurst was a daring, courageous woman and a leading suffragette. Together with her mother, Emmeline Pankhurst, she organized and led the Women's Social and Political Union (WSPU) and is remembered today as one of the most famous women in the fight for the vote.

Christabel, the eldest of Mrs Pankhurst's three daughters, grew up in a lively, political household. In 1902 Christabel enrolled at law school, a daring move when women were not allowed to be lawyers. However, her knowledge of the legal system was to prove useful in later years.

Emmeline and Christabel Pankhurst were a remarkable team. While Emmeline inspired the Union, it was Christabel who led it and who planned nearly all of the dramatic militant actions which continually caught the public eye. She was arrested and imprisoned many times, the first time in 1905, when she was thrown out of Manchester Free Trade Hall and pretended to spit at a policeman in order to be arrested and gain publicity.

By 1906, she had taken her law examination and was able to defend herself admirably in court. One of her finest moments was in 1908, when she was arrested and charged with 'conduct likely to cause a breach of the peace'. She appeared at Bow Street Court, London, and herself cross-examined Lloyd George, then Chancellor of the Exchequer, and Herbert Gladstone. Referring to a comment made by Gladstone's father (the famous Liberal Prime Minister), that without violence people would hardly have won any freedom, Christabel cleverly justified her actions.

In 1912, however, faced with a charge of conspiracy, she was forced to flee from England to France. Here she took the false name of Amy Roberts. She continued to organize and direct the suffragette campaign from Paris, by sending orders and instructions across the Channel through her friend Annie Kenney.

In 1914, when the First World War broke out, Christabel turned her energies from the vote to war work. After the war, when the vote for women was won, and women gained the right to stand as MPs, Christabel stood as a parliamentary candidate. She was not successful in becoming an MP, and after some years she went to the USA, where she spent the rest of her life.

Christabel defends herself in court in 1908, as her mother Emmeline looks on.

6

The War Years

1914-1918

The outbreak of the First World War in August 1914 can be seen as a turning point for many people in Britain. It accelerated the changes taking place in women's lives, but when it began no one knew just how important the war was going to be for women.

A wave of patriotism swept over the country, with thousands of young men eager to help in the fighting. As most people believed that the war would be over by Christmas, many men worried that

Below Mechanics working on an Avro Biplane during the First World War. Despite the views of some men, women proved themselves just as capable in these areas of work.

Sylvia Pankhurst speaking at a public meeting. She was bitterly opposed to Britain's part in the First World War.

they would miss their chance to fight for their country. In a similar spirit of patriotism, the suffragettes immediately stopped all their militant activities, and in return the government released all those in prison under a pardon. On behalf of the NUWSS, Millicent Fawcett declared 'let us prove ourselves worthy of citizenship, whether our claim is recognized or not'.

At first, there was confusion everywhere, and it seemed that women's role in the war would be confined to nursing and relief work, and 'keeping the home fires burning' while the men went off to battle. But the First World War was like no other war. Within months the Western Front settled down into trench warfare. The periods of stalemate, disrupted by sudden assaults, placed a terrible strain on the British army. More and more untrained soldiers poured into the front lines to replace the hundreds of casualties, leaving terrible gaps in the workforces at home.

On posters everywhere in Britain, the stern face of the War Minister Lord Kitchener proclaimed: 'Your country needs YOU!' The poster was aimed at men, but what the country really needed to win the struggle was its women. By early 1915, women were being called on to take over men's jobs so that more troops could be poured into the bloodbath on the Western Front. Women responded to this call for help in their thousands.

In some industries, such as the cotton mills of Lancashire, large numbers of women had always worked. Now, women were turning up in places where, in the male view, they had no right or ability to be. Women set to work in carpenters' workshops, metal-working factories, the docks, the railways and as conductors and drivers on buses.

They were resented. The unions were particularly bitter. They saw the improvements that they had gained in pay made 'less worthy' as unskilled female labour easily took to the work of skilled men. In many factories, men at first refused to co-operate with women, or to train them. The government got round this by promising (for some industries) that there would be no low female wages to undercut the male workers. Piece work rates would be the same for men *and* women. It was a fundamental step forward for women, who in the past had always received lower wages than men.

In some industries, however, female labour was still badly underpaid. Sylvia Pankhurst, who was bitterly opposed to the war, and the patriotic stance taken by her sister and mother, exposed some of the shocking conditions of employment and low pay in her paper *The Dreadnought*. Sylvia was not the only suffrage supporter to make her opinions known about the war. Many leading women within the suffrage campaign actively opposed the war. They were attacked by the press and regarded as traitors, but their work resulted in the

A munitions worker. During the war, women were asked to volunteer for work in factories and munitions plants. Even Emmeline Pankhurst encouraged women's role in the war effort, and women responded in their thousands.

formation of peace groups throughout the world, and laid the basis for the peace movements that still exist today.

However, most women supported the war effort and responded with enthusiasm. An appeal by Lloyd George, the Minister of Munitions, for women to make the guns and shells so urgently needed was backed by Emmeline Pankhurst, who was anxious to show the solidarity of women in the national crisis. Her encouragement drew thousands of volunteers. By the end of the war, 722,000 women, both married and single, were working in aircraft, chemical, and munitions industries, as well as helping to build ships and make iron and steel. They cheerfully put up with irregular meals, night shifts and poor accommodation, glad to be doing 'their bit' to help the men in the trenches.

Besides the women in the factories, thousands of others worked in offices, banks and the civil service. Middle-class women, who never before dreamed of earning a living, took clerical posts, and enjoyed them. Women doctors such as Dr Louisa Garrett Anderson and Dr Flora Murray opened and ran hospitals in France and elsewhere on the Continent. Before the war, their skills had been unwanted. Now, they were also invited to open and staff a military hospital in London.

By 1917, it became necessary for women to be employed in the forces as well – as cooks, drivers, clerical workers and dozens of other behind-the-lines roles. Three corps were formed – the Women's Army Auxiliary Corps, the Women's Royal Naval Service and, in 1918, the Women's Royal Air Force Service. The famous Land Army was also formed. Thousands of women volunteered to help on farms throughout the country whose male workforce had been 'sent to war'.

One of the most important results of such large-scale employment was that many women who had never earned money before, felt a new-found independence. They enjoyed having their *own* money to spend.

All these developments gave women increased power. One example came in 1915, when landlords on Clydeside tried to raise rents to an unjustly high level. Women took a leading part in the opposition to the rent increases, and the attempts by the landlord to take the tenants to court. Their indignation and actions gained the attention of the government, who quickly stepped in to control such rent increases.

> *Street-meetings, back-court meetings, drums, bells, trumpets – every method was used to bring the women out and organize them for the struggle. Notices were printed by the thousand and put up in the windows, wherever you went you could see them. In street after street scarcely a window without one, 'WE ARE NOT PAYING INCREASED RENT.'* Quoted in *Women's Voice*, No 1, 1971.

In 1916, the time to press the case of votes for women came when the government began to consider what to do about the out-of-date electoral register. Plans were put forward for a new register, based on war service. At once, the NUWSS pointed out that if such a register was made, women, who were also engaged in war work, must be included. The suffrage campaign was started again, although in a much quieter way. Women pressed their case through their MPs and by direct appeals to the Cabinet. They were supported by increasing numbers of men, and finally Asquith himself gave way, saying he could no longer deny women their claim.

There were many long drawn out meetings. To begin with, the proposal was for women to receive the vote at the age of 35. This was not on equal terms with men, who were allowed to vote at 21, but the NUWSS, on the advice of the Labour Party and sympathetic MPs, agreed to a higher age limit, as long as it was reduced to 30 years of age. This was accepted, and on 7 February 1918, the Representation of the People Bill, giving women of 30 and over the vote, was passed. The first battle had been won. But there was still a campaign to fight.

Below This cartoon from Punch *magazine shows that when women were finally given the vote in 1918, it was only granted to women over the age of 30.*

"WELL, SO YOU'RE GOING TO HAVE THE VOTE AT LAST."

"OH, ONLY WOMEN OVER THIRTY, YOU KNOW."

7

Victory and Disappointment

1918-1939

Above A woman in the 1918 General Election casts her vote for the very first time.

The General Election of 1918, the first for eight years, was both an exciting and disappointing time for women in politics. Now that male politicians had accepted that women would be voting, they began to take more notice of their views. Parliament easily passed a series of exciting laws that improved women's rights. One, proposed by the Government itself, gave women the right to stand for, and sit, in Parliament. Seventeen women stood for Parliament for the first time ever, including Christabel Pankhurst. All were defeated except for Countess Markievicz. Markievicz, an Irish Republican, was an extraordinary woman who had played a leading part in Ireland's struggle for self-rule and independence from Britain. But, since she refused to take the 'oath of allegiance' to Britain and her sovereign, she was not allowed to sit in Parliament.

Women had to wait until a by-election in 1919 to see the first woman, Viscountess Nancy Astor, enter the House of Commons as an MP. By 1923, there were eight women in Parliament. And, there were many more women holding important seats in local government. Women began to play an increasingly large part in the political parties too, and in 1919, the Sex Disqualification (Removal) Act allowed women to enter the fields of the civil service and law, to serve on juries and to become justices of the peace. Hannah Mitchell, a leading figure in politics in Manchester, was appointed a magistrate in 1926, and served on the City Council for eleven years.

Now that the first doors of women's emancipation had swung wide, more were opened. Gradual moves towards further equality did occur, although to many of those who had campaigned so long for women's rights, the rate of change was frustratingly slow. The civil service agreed to give women equal opportunities, but somehow in practice women did not get very far up the promotion ladder. Oxford University finally agreed to award women degrees, (before this, women had been allowed to attend lectures and take examinations, but they could not be awarded a degree at the end of the course). Cambridge University held out on this issue until 1948. New laws also began to improve women's position in relation to property rights, guardianship of children, maintenance and adoption of children

The Irish Republican, Countess Markievitz was the first elected MP, but refused to take her seat.

and widow's pensions.

The decision to give men the vote at the age of 21, and withhold it from women until the age of 30, was rapidly revealed as an absurdity. In 1928, Parliament passed, by a large majority, a law to remove this distinction. Even so, there was an attempt by some MPs to oppose the law on the grounds that young women were too frivolous and dangerous to be trusted with the vote. They pointed to women's short hair, short skirts, silk stockings and widespread use of make-up as their evidence. Their efforts failed.

On paper, women appeared to have won their campaign. So many improvements had been achieved. However, in reality there was still much more to be done. When the war ended and the men came back from being soldiers to return to their old lives, the women who had contributed so greatly to the outcome of the war, were suddenly described as 'blacklegs', keeping men out of their rightful jobs. Industry shed its women as fast as it could. Some women gave up their jobs with willing co-operation. Other women, however, felt used. If they fought to keep their jobs, they were described as selfish.

With the fight for women's suffrage over, women's organizations had to change to represent broader aims. The NUWSS altered its name to become the National Union of Societies for Equal Citizenship (NUSEC). Its new role was to campaign for the further advancement of equal rights for women. Millicent Fawcett was succeeded by Eleanor Rathbone, an ardent campaigner for the introduction of family allowances. For most of the 1920s, the various women's political movements, such as the NUSEC and the Women's Co-operative Guild, worked peacefully and optimistically together in an atmosphere produced by the victories already won. But differing attitudes and aims developed. More conventional feminists, sought merely to end the legal injustices which women suffered. Other more radical feminists wanted to go further.

Below A Women's Co-operative Guild banner. After the vote was won, the Guild continued to work for the needs of working women.

6

Our fifty years of struggle for the women's vote was not actuated [motivated] by our setting extraordinary value on the mere power of making a mark on a ballot paper every three or four years ... we valued it not as a ribbon to stick on our coat, but for the sake of equal laws, the enlarged opportunities and improved status for women which we knew it involved.
Millicent Fawcett, as President of the NUWSS.

9

Left Eleanor Rathbone at a meeting of the newly formed National Union of Societies for Equal Citizenship (NUSEC).

In her presidential speech to the NUSEC in 1926, Eleanor Rathbone called for changes in the structure of society to give women their true independence. She wanted the government to give wives and mothers family allowance, as this would make them independent and remove the very old argument that men needed higher pay than women because they had families to support.

The Wall Street Stock Market Crash in the USA, in 1929, triggered the Depression, and sent unemployment in Britain soaring to record levels. This, coupled with the growing threat of another war, made women's fight for equal pay and equal rights almost impossible to achieve. Instead, hundreds of women joined and supported the Hunger Marches of the 1930s. Two women, Maud Brown and Lily Webb, led a women's section in a hunger march in 1932, while the most famous hunger march of all, made by 200 men from Jarrow on Tyneside in 1936, was led by the red-headed Labour MP, Ellen Wilkinson (nicknamed 'Red Ellen'). Two years later, the threat of war, which had been in the background ever since 1918, suddenly came to the fore.

Above left Women were very much involved in the hunger marches of 1930s. Here, the women's contingent of a march in 1932 are pictured on their arrival in London from Lancashire.

Inset Ellen Wilkinson leads the Jarrow March in 1936.

Hannah Mitchell (1871–1956)

Hannah Mitchell was born into a poor farming family in Derbyshire. She was the fourth of six children and in her autobiography, *The Hard Way Up*, she says that she thinks she became a feminist at the age of eight, when she had to darn her brothers' socks, while they read or played dominoes.

Life was hard for her family. As a daughter, Hannah was expected to help her mother clean, cook, sew and wash, often working for as long as sixteen hours a day. She was passionately fond of books, but her mother needed her help at home, so Hannah left school after only two weeks. At fourteen, after a disagreement with her mother, she ran away from home.

Hannah first worked as a maid and then as a seamstress in a clothing 'sweatshop' [workshop]. Despite the long hours, Hannah educated herself, by reading and studying whenever she got the time. She was keenly aware of the social injustices in Britain, and began to develop an interest in socialism. She joined the Independent Labour Party (ILP) and despite being 'very nervous' addressed a number of political meetings.

Hannah was always aware of the inequality of women, and was an ardent supporter of votes for women. She met the Pankhursts in Manchester and soon became deeply involved with the suffragette movement, arranging meetings and recruiting support in the north of England. However, Hannah realized that suffragette activity was extremely difficult for working-class women with domestic responsibilities. She once said 'No cause was ever won between dinner and tea, and those of us who were married had to fight with one hand tied behind our backs ...'

In 1923, she was elected to sit on Manchester City Council, and for eleven years worked with

Hannah Mitchell was a leading figure in local politics in Manchester, and later became a magistrate.

a small group of dedicated women (including Ellen Wilkinson, later to be the first woman Minister of Education). In 1926, she was also appointed as a magistrate, a position she held until her retirement in 1946.

Hannah was a remarkable, determined woman, who always kept her links with working-class people and women in particular. She understood the pressures put on working-class women from her own experiences ... 'home life was ... a constant round of wash days, cleaning days, cooking and serving meals ... and the most sympathetic man can never be made to understand that meals do not come up through the tablecloth but have to be planned, bought and cooked ...'

Her great ambition was to be a writer, and she often regretted her lack of opportunity. After her death a manuscript was discovered, which had been written in secret. It was Hannah's autobiography. Entitled *The Hard Way Up* it was published in 1977 by Virago Press, and gives a remarkable picture of one working-class woman's political life.

8

War and Welfare

1939-1960

By the late 1930s many feminists, among them Eleanor Rathbone and Dora Russell, were devoting much of their time to international affairs and campaigning for peace. The Women's Co-operative Guild in particular (who introduced the white poppy in 1933), was, and still is, deeply committed to the peace movement. Many former suffrage workers had also become active in the League of Nations, the international peace-keeping organization set up in 1920. None of their efforts, however, could avert the coming world conflict.

The Spanish Civil War of 1936 had demonstrated to everybody that air raids would bring the brutalities of the coming war to the Home Front. As 1938 drew to a close, the Home Secretary made plans for the recruitment of a volunteer force of women to help safeguard defence at home. The result was the Women's Voluntary Service (WVS), a part-time organization that was started with five members, and within a few months was 300,000 strong.

As the war began in 1939, the Government put into action their policy to evacuate as many children as possible from the crowded cities. In three days, 1,250,000 children, some with their mothers, but most alone, were moved from the crowded, familiar streets to the countryside. Most of the arrangements for this massive exodus were carried out by the WVS, who coped with efficiency and care. The WVS went on throughout the war to provide help and welfare for thousands of refugees from Europe, who poured into the country from 1940.

Though many women were willing enough to come forward for such voluntary work, there was at first a greater reluctance to become involved in war work in the factories than there had been in the First World War. For one thing, there were fewer women in unpleasant occupations, such as domestic service, who would welcome the change. For another, it seemed to many people, and especially the government, that if men were to be conscripted for national service, then so should women.

In 1941, all women between the ages of 16 and 49 were registered, and could be directed into civilian jobs, unless they were pregnant, had children under the age of fourteen, or had other major domestic

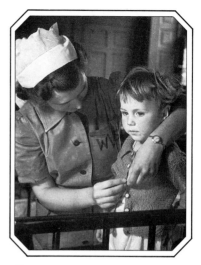

Above *A WVS member cares for an evacuee.*

Below *In the Second World War women were encouraged to enlist for national service.*

She's the girl
That makes the thing
That drills the hole
That holds the spring
That drives the rod
That turns the knob
That works the thingumebob ...
That's going to win the war.
Popular World War II song.

Manufacturing parts for bombers during the Second World War. Although women once again entered munitions factories in their thousands, they were less enthusiastic than in the First World War.

Before the war you didn't get a lot of married women working. When the war came ... we were happy working. I don't think we ever went back to the fireside in the same way again. Ivy Jones, *What did you do in the war, Mum?*, Age Exchange Publications.

ties. Single women were liable for conscription into the forces of civil defence (where they formed a quarter of the corps), unless they were in essential jobs such as nursing or the Land Army. Service with the forces was not in active combat, but in support work such as vehicle maintenance and repair, driving and radar control. Women were also trained to use anti-aircraft guns, searchlights and barrage balloons.

By 1943, nine out of ten single women were in the forces or industry; and about three million married women and widows were working, which was more than double the pre-war figure. There were over 1,870,000 women in trade unions. The need for married women to work resulted in a huge demand for day nurseries, which the WVS provided.

The Second World War disrupted the lives of all women, not just those in the forces or those doing war work. Women had to cope with rationing, shortages of essential goods and the blackout. Clothes were rationed, and it was not possible to have more than one new set of clothes a year, if that. The end of the war in 1945 brought no end to the hard times. In fact, for a time it grew worse as American aid stopped.

Readjusting to life in peacetime was difficult for women who had grown used to the excitement of wartime, the independence of earning money, and life away from the dull routine of housework. But, women workers were now in a stronger position than at the end of the First World War. They had had some success in gaining equal rights, and in 1943, the trade unions agreed that women workers should have equal rights to employment. They also agreed that the sex of a person should not be the guideline for the amount of money paid for a job. Another very important move in 1944, meant that it was illegal to sack a teacher when she married.

The coming to power of a Labour Government at the end of the war in 1945 also brought more positive moves toward women's independence. The government wanted to put into practice the proposals for a welfare state, along the guidelines contained in the Beveridge Report of 1942. The welfare state became a reality in 1948, with the setting up of the National Health Service and other schemes for social benefit. Of particular importance to women was the introduction of the family allowance, which had been a brain-child of many feminists in the inter-war years. Family allowance, payable for each child except the first, was originally given to the fathers! After a barrage of criticism from women everywhere, the family allowance payment was paid directly to the mothers.

The 1950s saw a return to the fashion of early marriages, and the government encouraged women's role as 'home-maker'. A 'baby boom' occurred and the press continually stressed the importance of maternal care in the early years of childhood. Women did manage to attain equal pay for teachers and civil servants, but by the 1960s it seemed that the involvement of women in politics had run out of steam.

After the Second World War, women were encouraged to stay at home once more, as the role of 'home-maker' and mother was now seen as the most important goal.

Dora Russell (1894–1987)

Dora Russell was born into a middle-class family. She had a happy childhood and a good education. She wanted to be an actress, but instead won a scholarship to Girton College, University of Cambridge. At that time, Cambridge did not award degrees to women, but women were allowed to attend classes. While at university, she began to rebel against the Edwardian views of women. She was extremely shocked by the events of the First World War and became a life-long pacifist and peace campaigner.

During the 1920s, Dora Russell became active in the campaign to make birth control more available to women. In 1921, Marie Stopes opened the first British birth control clinic and Dora fought for local authority clinics to be set up in more cities. She met with much opposition.

The Women's Co-operative Guild, however, was staunchly in favour of birth control, particularly for poor women who suffered many pregnancies. By 1930, the work of Stopes and Russell could be seen to have had some effect – the Ministry of Health had begun to allow local authorities to provide limited birth control advice.

While involved in this campaign, Dora Russell also wrote *Hypatia; or Women and Knowledge*. In it Dora demanded a woman's right to control her own body. For her, it seemed unacceptable that men, who do not bear children, should have any say about child-bearing or contraception.

By the 1930s, Dora was also campaigning for the rights of women to have an abortion, which at the time was absolutely illegal. In 1936, together with Stella Browne, they helped to found the Abortion Law Reform Association.

During the 1950s, Dora became actively involved in the Campaign for Nuclear Disarmament (CND), and in 1958 she led the Women's Caravan for Peace across the whole of Europe, to protest against the 'Cold War' that existed between the USA and the USSR.

In an interview in 1982, she said that she firmly believed that women were the carers in society and that their nurturing and caring has been taken advantage of. She also said '... we don't want women to stop acting like women, what we want is the reverse. We can't afford to have any more people with anti-life values. It is men who have to stop acting like men and start acting like women ... we do not know what sort of society women would have shaped for their contribution has never been allowed ...'

Left *Dora Russell was active in politics all her adult life, and was particularly involved in issues such as birth control and nuclear disarmament.*

9

Liberating Women

1960-1980

In 1963, an American women, Betty Friedan, published an important book, *The Feminine Mystique*, which described the image of womanhood that was being promoted to American women. She showed how women's magazines, advertising and education were encouraging women to follow traditional roles of marriage and motherhood. But, more importantly, Friedan also found that many American women were suffering from what she called 'a problem with no name'. Despite their comfortable home lives, a great deal of women were dissatisfied.

The book was an immediate best-seller. It marked the emergence of a second wave of feminist feeling, and reflected women's need to become more closely involved in all aspects of politics once more. The Women's Liberation Movement developed from this, in the USA, during the exciting years of the sixties. Students, young people, black and white, began to demand equal rights and opportunities.

The Women's Liberation Movement first came to public attention in 1968, when women demonstrated against the Miss America pageant in New Jersey. They believed that such events degraded women. They argued that the contest treated women as 'objects', rather than intelligent equals. It was an argument first voiced some 170 years before by Mary Wollstonecraft, who protested that women were 'the toys of man'. The next day, the newspapers were full of the demonstration. Most of the newspaper articles criticized the women, who were described as 'bra burners', an insult that showed no understanding of the protest but was used for some years.

Despite the criticism, the movement grew rapidly, spreading first to Canada and then to Britain. The 1960s were years of economic boom, and this led to a great availability of jobs, especially in white-collar work and welfare work. Women in such positions were finding that conditions were not equal at all. In Britain, the National Council of Labour Women produced a report on discrimination against women and there was an upsurge of militancy by women workers. This began when 187 women sewing machinists at Ford's car plant in Dagenham went on strike to gain an up-grading of their work. The strike ended when the women accepted just 92 per cent of the male wage.

Above Germaine Greer. Her book, The Female Eunuch, *published in Britain in 1971, was influential in making women think more about their position in society.*

Below 1976: Jayaben Desai prepares to go to the picket line at Grunwick photographic processing factory in Middlesex. The strikers included many Asian women, who were fighting for the right to become members of a trade union.

By 1969, many British towns had Women's Liberation groups. In March 1970, the first national conference took place at Ruskin College, Oxford. Originally, it was arranged by some historians to be a small study group, but it was so popular, that finally 600 women came to attend. A number of resolutions were passed, which later became known as the 'seven demands'. They included equal pay for equal work; equal education and job opportunities; free contraception and abortion; an end to discrimination against lesbians; free 24-hour child care and the legal and financial independence of women.

During the 1970s, women's involvement in the movement grew rapidly. From discussion groups, a new slogan – 'The Personal is Political' – came about. Its theory argues that women's personal feelings *are* political statements. Up until this time, women's personal lives and their lives at home, were viewed merely as 'emotional' experiences. The theory demands that issues such as family care and childbearing should be recognized as political issues. What happens to women at home is just as important as what happens to them in the outside world.

There was an explosion of ideas in books, pamphlets and at meetings. One of the most influential books at the time was called *The Female Eunuch*. Published in Britain in 1971, it was written by an Australian, Germaine Greer. She argued that women's roles as mothers and wives prevented them from reaching their full potential, in terms of work and education. She felt women should not get married, then they would be totally free to do the best they possibly could. The 1970s were years of tremendous activity as women became involved in politics through pressure groups and campaigns. Issues such as health, abortion, homosexuality, racism and

Below *Women's Liberation demonstrations such as this were common during the early 1970s. The demands being made included equal pay and job opportunities.*

pornography pulled women together to try and change things. These years saw the setting up of rape crisis centres, lesbian support groups and refuges for battered wives. Issues facing disabled men and women were also brought to the public's attention. Improvement in health issues, such as contraception, pregnancy and childbirth resulted in the creation of free family planning services in 1975 and breast cancer screening in 1978.

Women also continued to fight for more traditional equal rights both within Parliament and at work. Following the Dagenham strike in 1968, the TUC agreed to support industrial action for equal pay. Pressure from sympathetic MPs and trade unions eventually led to the Equal Pay Act becoming law in 1970. Despite this, differences between men's and women's earnings continued. (Even today, it has been estimated that on average women earn only about 70 per cent of men's wages.)

Other legislation to improve women's position included the Sex Discrimination Act, in 1975, which made it unlawful to discriminate on the grounds of sex in employment, education, and in the provision of homes, goods and services. Other improvements at work gave women maternity leave and pay, with the right to go back to the same job, once the child was born. Such legislation was included in the Employment Protection Act.

It would be misleading to think that all the positive steps forward for women's equality were merely the result of the activities of the Women's Liberation Movement. Without the commitment and hard work of earlier political groups such as the Women's Co-operative Guild, the suffrage movements and NUSEC, to name a few, such legislation would not have come about.

> *Women do two-thirds of the world's work, for less than 10 per cent of the world's salary, and own less than 1 per cent of the world's wealth.* United Nations Statistic, 1980.

Above Conservative leader Margaret Thatcher, Britain's first woman Prime Minister, and by January 1988, the longest serving Prime Minister in Britain this century.

10

The 1980s

During the 1980s, women's involvement in politics changed. To some extent, it moved away from radical feminism towards challenging the changed political and economic climate of the 1980s. Unemployment and a world recession brought many problems to a large number of people in Britain.

In 1979, a Conservative Government came to power. It was headed by Margaret Thatcher, Britain's first woman Prime Minister. It was an achievement that would have been unthinkable just 100 years ago. However, not all women who enter politics support the aims of the women's movement, and equality for women. Under successive Conservative Governments, there has been a return to the Victorian idea that 'a woman's place is in the home'.

Since 1979, the economic recession and a serious shortage of jobs have led to many women being forced to stay at home, rather than work. Financial cutbacks in the health service and other social services have put a further strain on women's responsibilities at home, as has the closure of nursery schools and day-care centres through lack of money.

Women were active in resisting certain pieces of Conservative

Right Miners' wives helped to lead the fight against pit closures, during the 1984/5 miners' strike. They organized public meetings and demonstrations. For many it was their first political experience.

legislation, for example, the new laws introduced to curtail the power of trade unions. During the 1984/5 miners' strike, miners' wives and partners held public meetings, stood on picket lines, ran soup kitchens, addressed rallies and travelled the length and breadth of Britain and abroad seeking support and raising funds. In 1986, Brenda Dean, head of the printers' union SOGAT '82, was elected to lead her union against the newspaper magnate Rupert Murdoch. In January and February 1988, nurses in a number of hospitals challenged tradition and came out on strike for the first time ever to protest against the lack of funds given to the National Health Service.

Women have also been very involved in campaigns against American nuclear weapons being based in Britain, particularly the women of Greenham Common. In 1981, the news that Cruise missiles were to be sited in Britain caused a small group of people to march from Cardiff, Wales to the United States Air Force base at Greenham Common, Berkshire, where the missiles were to arrive. The march arrived at Greenham on 5 September 1981, and a permanent peace camp was set up outside the base.

Eventually, women set up camps at all the different gates around the perimeter fence, naming them after the colours of the rainbow – yellow, blue, green, purple and so on. The fame of the Greenham Women's Peace Camp and the determination of the women who lived there in often appalling conditions, facing daily arrests, soon spread throughout the world.

Despite the arrival of the missiles in 1983, the peace camp grew. The women used effective non-violent way to put their point across, including drama and theatre. One of their most memorable actions was in December 1984, when 50,000 women and men held hands and encircled the base to illustrate the support their cause had

Brenda Dean, head of SOGAT '82.

6━━━━━━━━

Greenham has changed the lives of many women. Traditionally men have left home for the front-line of war. Now women are leaving home to work for peace . . . Peace isn't just about moving a few pieces of war-furniture . . . it is about the condition of our lives. Our whisperings must now be shouted. Greenham Common: Women at the Wire, *edited by Barbara Harford and Sarah Hopkins, 1984.*

━━━━━━━━**9**

Left *December 1984: Thousands of women link arms to form a human chain around Greenham Common Air Force Base in Berkshire. They were protesting against the siting of American nuclear Cruise missiles in Britain.*

gained. In December 1987, an agreement was signed between General Secretary Gorbachev of the USSR and President Reagan of the USA, whereby Cruise missiles were to be removed from Europe. Nevertheless, Greenham women announced their intention to stay until the very last missile left.

Women in politics have also continued to fight in and through Parliament as well. In 1979, when Margaret Thatcher was elected, only 19 women were returned to the House of Commons – out of a total of 635 MPs. The 1979 results were the worst for nearly 30 years, but even in previous elections, there had never been more than 5 per cent of women MPs. This is quite staggering, particularly as women make up 52 per cent of the voting population.

In 1980, a new women's organization was set up to try to improve this situation. The '300 Group', as it is called, aims to get that number of women into the House of Commons. They look at why there are still so few women in Parliament, and have found a number of reasons. Despite women's long political history, women who want to enter Parliamentary politics as a career face many obstacles, among them lack of confidence, lack of money and unusual working hours which conflict with family responsibilities.

Since 1980, the '300 Group' has continued to encourage and work for women to enter Parliament, but they recognize that far-reaching changes are needed before it can be a real possibility for most women.

The 1987 General Election brought more women than ever before into Parliament. For the first time there were 41 women MPs. They include women such as Edwina Currie, Theresa Gorman, Lynda Chalker, all Conservative MPs, and, in the Labour Party, women such as Jo Richardson, Clare Short and Diane Abbott, Britain's first black woman MP. The SDP also returned Rosie Barnes and the Liberal Party returned Ray Michie. Many of them were new to Parliament and have quite differing views on women's rights. Edwina Currie, for instance, has spurned issues particular to women and feminism; others like Maria Fyfe, MP for Glasgow Maryhill, and Clare Short, MP for Birmingham Ladywood are deeply committed to women's rights.

Despite this number of women MPs, women's rights remain under threat. During the 1980s, the introduction of Clause 28 in the Local Authority Bill, has been viewed as a threat to lesbian and homosexual rights. In 1988, David Alton's Private Members' Bill, proposed to introduce a legal time limit on abortions of 18 weeks. Many people felt that such a move would threaten a woman's right to choose and to have control over her own body. The Bill caused more than 10,000 women to march through London in protest on 19 March 1988.

Below Ray Michie, Liberal MP (now Social and Liberal Democrats MP). In the 1987 General Election 41 women became Members of Parliament.

Joan Ruddock (1943)

Joan Ruddock, presently one of the 41 women MPs in the House of Commons, has had a varied and interesting political career, and has always been involved in leading the fight for change.

Born in Pontypool, South Wales, Joan is from a working-class family. She was educated at Pontypool Grammar School and at Imperial College, University of London, where she gained a degree in Botany and Chemistry. From her teenage years, Joan had been interested in politics, and in 1970 became a member of the Labour Party.

In her early political days, Joan's work was concerned with issues such as homelessness, youth unemployment and civil rights. From 1968, she worked for SHELTER, the charity that helps the homeless, and was made Director of the Oxfordshire Housing Aid centre. In 1973, she became the special programmes adviser helping young unemployed people, and also spent some years as organizer for Reading Citizens' Advice Bureau.

Throughout her career, Joan has been a member of a number of pressure groups, and is especially committed to the Campaign for Nuclear Disarmament (CND). She was elected chairperson of CND in 1981. Since then, her untiring work – addressing meetings, leading marches and lobbying Parliament – has helped to keep the nuclear issue in the public eye. In 1984, she received the Frank Cousins Peace Award for her contribution to the peace movement.

In the General Election of June 1987, Joan Ruddock was elected as MP for Lewisham Deptford in London. She has continued to fight for women's equality and encourage women's involvement in Parliament, although she believes that the unorthodox working hours of the House of Commons, among other things, does tend to exclude women with family responsibilities!

Despite all her many commitments as an MP, Joan still finds time to give her support to CND. In April 1988, she joined a deputation of women MPs who met with NATO Ministers in Brussels, to discuss arms limitations.

Joan Ruddock's diverse, successful political career is a fine example of women's contribution to the world of politics.

Joan Ruddock, MP for Lewisham Deptford, has had a very successful political career.

11

The Future

This Women's Co-operative Guild banner shows two women clasping hands. Unity is an important principle of women's politics, and no doubt this will continue, whatever changes women campaign for in the future.

> **I cannot imagine a life that did not have an element of campaigning, of trying to bring about some change and of trying to help people to gain what is rightfully theirs.** Joan Ruddock, 1982.

Today, it is hard to know what the future is for women and politics. More than 150 years of campaigning has achieved a great deal. Women in Britain today are physically healthier than their Victorian foremothers. They have smaller families, more freedom and wider job and education opportunities than might ever have been expected 100 years ago.

Schools, colleges and universities are equally open to women. Women such as Anna Ford have opened up broadcasting; others such as Anita Roddick of The Body Shop, have shown women can be successful in business too. There are peers in the House of Lords, women councillors, judges, bus drivers, engineers and plumbers. Maternity benefits, birth control, the right to divorce, and of course, the right to vote, have now all been granted.

Women's involvement in politics, both through campaigning pressure groups and Parliament is here to stay, and it is no longer regarded by most people as either peculiar or outrageous. But, despite many positive achievements, many battles are still to be won. While women make up 42 per cent of university students only 1 in 5 doctors is a woman. Most low-paid and part-time workers are women, and their earnings still lag behind men.

The question for many women today is, what is the best way to achieve further change? For some women, Parliament is not the answer, nor is gaining equality on terms decided by men. Some modern feminists believe that very little has improved for women, and women have to continue to struggle in a world where they do not make the most important decisions. Other modern feminists, such as Lynne Segal, argue that women *can* work through the existing society and Parliament.

Many women believe that they must continue to work for change through the traditional, established political power – that of trade unions, local councils and Parliament. The arguments are complicated, and there is probably no simple answer. Only the future will bring the answers, but, whatever the solution, women will lead the fight for change.

Projects

Women MPs and councillors

Find out from your town hall or borough council the name of the constituency where you live. Then, also from the town hall or borough council, find out who your local Member of Parliament is. Is your MP a woman? What political party does your MP stand for?

To find out more information about the different political parties, and about your MP, you can write to the party's information unit. Addresses for these can be found in your local library. Ask each party how many of their MPs are women. Then make a chart, listing the name of the political party at the top, with the names of women MPs in that particular party below.

Look through your local newspapers and try to find out if any of your local councillors are women. Alternatively, visit your town hall or borough council, which has a 'List of Councillors'. How many are women? Do you have a major or mayoress in your area?

A picture of the past

Oral history projects, like the one below, need some planning, but they are a fascinating way of building up a picture of the past, through the experience of someone who has lived in that period. Using a tape recorder, interview your grandmother or an elderly neighbour. Then, interview your mother, aunt or neighbour (around 30–45 years old). Decide on the questions you are going to ask beforehand, and make a careful note of them. After the interviews, use the recordings to write up the answers. Compare the two sets of answers. Are they similar or are there any noticeable differences? You can also compare your answers to those of pupils in your class. Below are some ideas:

Ask your grandmother/elderly neighbour:
* What was life like for you when you were in your teens?
* What differences did you see/experience between your life and the life of your brother/s or male friends?
* Did you learn about politics, Parliament and the political parties at school?
* Can you remember the first time you voted. If so, when was it?
* At what age did you marry? Was marriage the most likely possibility for you, or did you also take up a career?
* What were your experiences of the Second World War? Were you old enough to help out with factory work, or become a Land Girl, or drive a bus?
* How do you think life has changed for women today?

Ask your mother/aunt/neighbour:
* What was it like for you in your teens? Did you have as much freedom as young women today?
* Do you think that being a woman has made a difference to your opportunities in jobs, and in education?
* What jobs were you expected to help with around the house? Did they differ from those of your brother/s or male friends?
* Were you involved in, or can you remember any of the Women's Liberation marches in the late 1960s–1970s?
* Have you ever thought about becoming a local councillor, MP, or member of a PTA (Parent Teacher Association)?
* What are your views on women's struggle to get more women MPs into Parliament? Do you think it would be a good thing?

Books to Read

Books for younger readers

Adams, Carol *Ordinary Lives: A Hundred Years Ago* (Virago, 1982)

Beddoe, Deirdre *Discovering Women's History, A Practical Guide* (Pandora Press, 1983)

Beer, Reg *The Matchgirls: The fight against sweating in East London* (National Museum of Labour History, pamphlet No. 2)

Einhorn, Barbara *Let's Discuss Women's Rights* (Wayland, 1988)

Goldman, H *Emma Patterson* (Lawrence and Wishart, 1974)

Hollis, Patricia *Women in Public—The Women's Movement 1850–1900* (Allen and Unwin, 1979)

Kramer, Ann *A Suffragette* (Wayland, 1988)

Liddington, Jill and Norris, Jill *One Hand Tied Behind Us* (Virago, 1978)

Macdonald, Fiona *Working for Equality* (Virago, 1987)

Mitchell, Hannah *The Hard Way Up* (Virago, 1977)

Pugh, M *Women's Suffrage in Britain 1867–1929* (Historical Association Pamphlet, 1980)

Rodgers, Barbara *52%: Getting Women's Power into Politics* (Women's Press, 1983)

Snellgrove, L *Suffragettes and Votes for Women* (Longman, 1985)

Sproule, Anna *Solidarity* (Macdonald, 1987)

Books for older readers

Coote, Anna and Campbell, Beatrix *Sweet Freedom: The Struggle for Women's Liberation* (Picador, 1982)

Rowbotham, Sheila *Hidden from History* (Pluto, 1973)

Sanders, Deirdre and Read, Jane *Kitchen Sink or Swim: Women in the 80s* (Penguin, 1982)

Spender, Dale *There's always been a Women's Movement This Century* (Pandora Press, 1982)

Vallance, Elizabeth *Women in the House* (Athlone Press, 1979)

Glossary

Academic Concerned with intellectual, reasoned learning, rather than practical knowledge.

Cabinet The group of leading ministers from the government.

Campaigner A person who involves him/herself in public speaking and demonstrations to achieve a social, political or commercial goal.

Chartism A reform movement in Britain in the 1830s–1840s.

Companion Particularly in the past, a young woman who provided company for an elderly lady.

Constituencies Marked-out districts or areas to be represented by different MPs.

Degraded Reduced in worth, disgraced.

Democratic Upholding the ideas of democracy, whereby all the members of a group help in the decision making.

Devaluing Reducing the value or worth of something.

Discrimination Unfair, unjust treatment of a person or group of people on the grounds of sex, race, colour or religion.

Double standard A set of morals which allows one group of people to live with greater freedom than another group.

Economic recession A period of economic hardship in a country.

Enfranchisement The given power to vote.

Evaluate To judge the value or success.

Exploitation Make unfair use of, or take advantage of a person.

Family Allowance Former name for child benefit – a regular government payment to parents of children under a certain age.

Feminism A set of beliefs or a movement which advocates equal rights for women.

Feminist A supporter of feminism.

Glorify To make something more splendid or imposing than reality.

Governess A woman teacher, particularly in the past, employed in a private household to teach the children.

'Grass-root' activities Activities/actions which are concerned with issues that affect everyday life and ordinary people.

Hypocrisy Promoting a set of moral beliefs which are different from own behaviour.

Independent Free from the control of others.

Industrial Revolution A period of British history starting around the 1760s, in which the invention of a series of machines and implements, led to a revolution in the way goods were made.

Legislation The act of making laws.

Machine-breakers Workers, particularly textile workers in the early 1800s, who opposed the introduction of new machinery, so carried out raids to break the equipment. Also known as luddites.

Mouthpiece A magazine or publication which expresses the views and beliefs of an organization.

Opportunities Favourable, advantageous circumstances or prospects.

Oppression The control of a person by injustice or force;

Patriotism Devotion to one's country and concern for its defence.

Political prisoners People who are imprisoned for their political beliefs and conscience.

Potential Capability but not yet achieved.

Privileged Enjoying advantages, often financial, not shared by most people.

Propaganda An organized way of giving information to assist the cause of a government or movement.

Protective legislation Laws which were intended to safeguard health and safety at work.

Radical To change greatly.

Radical politics Politics which seek to change laws and the system of government a great deal.

Raiment Clothing.

Reform To change and improve laws.

Repealed A law which has been officially cancelled.

Resolutions Decisions made at public meetings.

Sanctity Being regarded as pure and free from sin.

Secret ballot A vote made in secret.

Self-rule Another word for self-government.

Socialism See 'socialist'.

Socialist A person who believes in socialism – whereby a country's wealth (land, industry, resources) should belong to the people as a whole, not to individual private owners, and the state should decide how such resources are used to the common good.

Solidarity Unity of interests.

Stereotype A standardized, artificial image or picture of a person or a way of life.

Suffrage The right to vote in elections.

Trade union An association of workers formed to bargain with the employer for better working conditions and pay.

Trivialized Made trivial or unimportant.

Turbulent In a confused, unruly state.

Unity The joining together of separate groups.

Venereal disease A disease passed on by sexual intercourse.

White-collar work Work which is non-manual, such as administrative or clerical.

Words in quotations

Differentiate To see a difference between.

Emancipation The act of freeing, or being liberated.

Fetters Chains fastened around ankles.

Index

Numbers in **bold** refer to illustrations